**> APAC 2018 Events**

## February
**Indochina** // Bangkok

Rapid-fire Solution Stage

Networking Sessions

## April
**Indonesia** // Jakarta
**Focus On** // Hyderabad

## June
**Enterprise** // Shanghai

Thought Leadership & Panels

Technology Showcases

## July
**Webscale** // Bangalore

## August
**Australia**// Sydney

## September
**South East Asia** // Singapore

Bespoke Sessions

Data Center Tours

## November
**Hyperscale** // Beijing
**Enterprise** // Mumbai
**Converged** // Hong Kong

**FREE for end-users,
scan to find out more:**

**The Region's Most Indepth Cloud & Data Center Infrastructure Transformation Event**

www.DCD.events
in f y #DCD

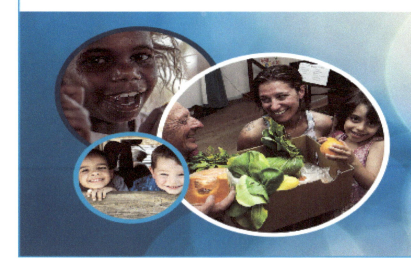

# Telecom Times

*A first-year anniversary issue*

*Compiled and edited by Richard van der Draay, editor and founder*

Telecom Times

First Printing: 2017

ISBN 978-0-244-03501-3

Telecom Times
PO Box 953, Gladesville, NSW 2111, Australia

www.telecomtimes.com.au

"Living well is the best revenge" – George Herbert, *The Temple*, 1633

*Proudly based in the Emerald City*

# CONTENTS

## PREFACE

## YEAR ONE IN PICTURES

## FROM THE PAGES OF TELECOM TIMES' YEAR ONE

## CONTRIBUTORS

# PREFACE

Just about a year on from the launch of Telecom Times, it seems an opportune moment to take stock and mark the occasion with the release of a veritable anniversary print magazine.

So much has happened during the past twelve months or so, which could well have shaped up to be an *annus horribilis* - and then some. On a more personal level, I found myself the startled recipient of a Parkinson's disease diagnosis just before Christmas (the ultimate real life deadline for my much-loved keyboard skills), and that was just the half of it.

Deciding from the outset to make the most of things, Telecom Times soon became a reality, with crucial early support emerging quite organically and swiftly, once a first rudimentary incarnation of the publication appeared on the scene.

The likes of Equinix Australia, F5 Networks and Motorola Solutions, to name but a few, believed in the (ad) venture from day one, and sponsored its attendance at some key overseas telco conferences.

And it simply wouldn't do to omit the instant unquestioning encouragement of PR legend Hannah Watterson and her incredible staff, one and all.

Communications Alliance CEO John Stanton was equally quick off the mark, personally ensuring the peak industry body was among the first paid subscribers on our books. Former NBN Co CTO and current co-owner of HKBN Gary McLaren, for his part, was very generous with his time when I interviewed him on the sidelines of the Broadband Forum Asia conference in Hong Kong.

The resulting Q&A style article generated some of the best metrics for the site in those early days. It is included in this print issue, along with a new feature penned by Gary. In late July, Telecom Times welcomed the landmark appointment of Senior Journalist Aimee Chanthadavong. And, just recently – coinciding with TT turning one year - we were able to help former Fairfax journalist Ben Grubb re-emerge from the depths of PR land, with Ben having come on board as Editor-At-Large.  At the time of writing, there are some more editorial staffing announcements being prepared.

Another key addition to the team as our Marketing Manager Edgardo Chua, who will be overseeing our media kit and marketing portfolio. Already, Edgardo's ideas and input have laid the foundations of what I'm sure will prove to be a solid, sound path forward for our humble venture.

And, while right now with the new editorial team firmly in place and our pressing marketing requirements starting to be addressed, it feels as though the current steep scaling up exercise we find ourselves in the midst of might actually end up somewhere.

Mind you, from the very start it was clear to me that what's on offer in TT by necessity would always have to be a snapshot of stories available on any given day. A handpicked bouquet of telco happenings if you like.  After all, there's no way we could comfortably cover the same extensive beats that some other ventures manage do without similar backing from major media companies.

Nor would I want to just breathlessly try to copy other telco-focused publications. There's no value in slavishly copying what appears to be working for others.  What I'm ultimately aiming for is to present a fresh, engaging publication, one which those with an interest in telecommunications enjoy reading for whatever reason.

So, let's focus on moving forward and continuing to build up the reach, depth and breadth of Telecom Times. The gods of telco, such as they are, know we could use a few more publications covering such captivating topics as cloud, SD-WAN, 5G, AI and Big Data, along with colocation and interconnection, submarine and satellite connectivity, UC and critical comms and yes... the NBN.

# Telecom Times turns one

By Craig Daveson in *Media News* on Wednesday, 20th September 2017

Richard van der Draay's Telecom Times is celebrating its first birthday this month, and is marking the occasion with new subscription options as well an on-demand print magazine.

Telecom Times was founded after van der Draay parted ways with CommsDay where he served as assistant editor from 2014 to 2016, and speaking to Influencing, van der Draay explained what the experience of starting his own telecoms publication has been like during the past year.

"I suppose it's always daunting to strike out on your own, no matter what field you're in. But then of course, in a way it might seem counter-intuitive to launch a brand new telco news outlet in the current volatile media climate. Especially with so many great telco journos leaving the profession for PR pastures new," said van der Draay.

"I think we've gone from strength to strength, right from day one. Along the way, I was incredibly heartened to see so much support and encouragement coming our way — at times from some rather surprising quarters."
"The thing about going out on a limb… is the complete freedom, which, inevitably, also instantly comes with an equal measure of unavoidable responsibility."

As markers for success over the past year, van der Draay says that forging media partnerships and also attending major jtelco events in Hong Kong such as the Broadband Asia Forum and Critical Communications were big milestones for Telecom Times to reach. "Aimee Chanthadavong coming on board as our senior journalist was another great stand-out moment," added van der Draay.

On launching a subscription service, van der Draay said that he has been testing the waters of monetisation, and will be tweaking Telecom Times' offering as time goes by.

"The bottom-line is that with limited resources, at least in terms of time and headcount, it becomes paramount to find a model that works and which — dare I say it — proves to be sustainable over time," said van der Draay.

"So, right now we have a blend of free access articles, premium content and a quite comprehensive range of advertising and marketing options. The idea is to keep building up the paid membership section, which currently already features more in-depth articles, a dedicated daily news feed and now also — stop press! — a premium online magazine digest service."

Plans for a physical product are also in the works, with a glossy on-demand magazine set to mark what van der Draay described as a "herculean effort" in keeping the publication alive for its first year.

*Pre-professional involvement website design DIY effort.*

**SUBSEA CABLES ARE THE FOUNDATION FOR GLOBAL DIGITAL BUSINESS**
Jeremy Deutsch, Equinix Australia Managing Director

Digital is transforming all industries and is the engine for growth. However, it is the arteries criss-crossing our seabeds around the world that enables telecommunications carriers and enterprises to capitalise on business opportunities.

It is important to remember that satellite links account for only a small percentage of international bandwidth traffic. The majority is carried by undersea cables running from beach to beach throughout our major oceans. A greater proliferation of these cables is essential in the digital age, as organisations depend on instant connectivity to people, locations, clouds and data worldwide.

Cloud growth is the newest wave of traffic driving the surge in data and is increasing the importance of subsea cables. Cloud providers and major content companies are now investors in new cables, as the demand for real-time access continues to grow and service providers need to stage content closer to end users.

The new wave of interconnections

With that in mind, it is no surprise that in recent years we have seen a spate of high-profile international subsea cable projects. According to SubTel Forum, 93,000 miles of cable was laid in 2016, more than in the last five years combined, and more than three and a half times the circumference of the earth at the equator.

That's why Equinix has ramped up strategic partnerships in subsea cable projects through our network of more than 180 data centres across five continents. Recently, we added a few more subsea cables directly into our data centres in Australia, some which bypass the additional hop through the traditional landing stations, and instead, terminate directly in a network and cloud rich colocation data centre, improving performance, increasing choice and lowering costs for all participants.

A good example of these new wave of cables is New Zealand-based subsea cable company Hawaiki Cable's 14,000-kilometre cable system will provide trans-Pacific connectivity between Australia, New Zealand and the United States.

That deal meant Hawaiki can offer Equinix data center customers direct access to the subsea cable.

Vocus Communications also recently announced that Equinix's international business exchange (IBX) data centres in Melbourne and Sydney will be used for metro pops for its Australian-Singapore Cable (ASC).

ASC, a four-pair fibre network with 100 wavelengths per pair, is expected to deliver at least 40 Tbps of capacity from Australia to Southeast Asia, and will provide a new route to the subcontinent from Western Australia. The level of high performance connectivity these cable links are providing between Australia and the rest of the world opens significant growth opportunities for Australian businesses.

## Hooking up the world

Equinix is home to 1,600+ networks and 2,750+ cloud and IT service providers on a global platform that now spans 44 markets on five continents and hosts more than 9,500 customers worldwide. These data centres are ideal landing points for submarine cable systems as they provide a neutral meeting point for networks, content providers, cloud providers and financial services providers to leverage these new interconnection options.

When subsea cable systems are linked to cloud and content ecosystems inside Equinix, businesses can access a variety of scalable cloud services almost anywhere they need to be.

A greater proliferation of subsea cables is essential in this digital age, at a time when organisations depend on instant connectivity to markets and partners worldwide. As subsea cables connect more places, they enable the low latency that real-time technologies like those supporting electronic trading and the Internet of Things require.

It's a fascinating and exciting time to be in telecommunications, and with digital transformation still top of everyone's agenda and data growing at rapid rates, Equinix congratulates Telecom Times on its first anniversary.

*Equinix SY4, the firm's latest Sydney data center.*

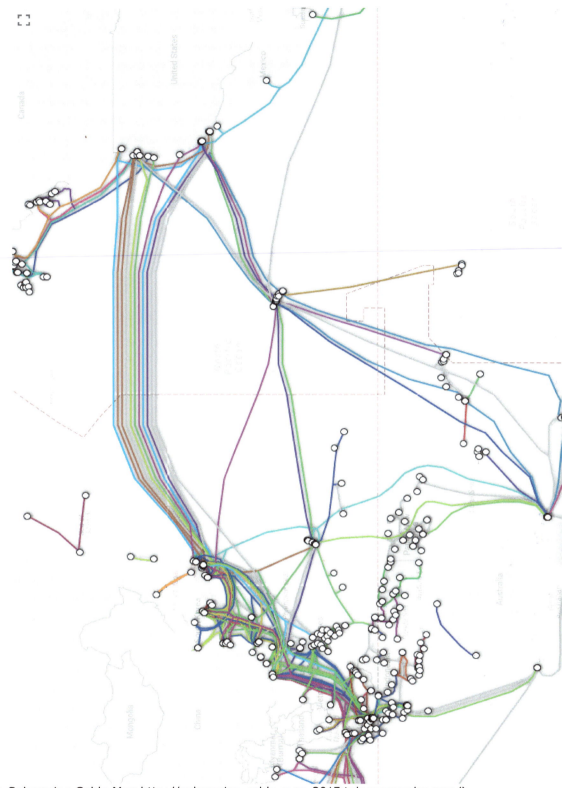

(Source: TeleGeography, Submarine Cable Map http://submarine-cable-map-2017.telegeography.com/)

## Q&A WITH GARY B. SMITH, PRESIDENT AND CEO OF CIENA

**Telecom Times:** What are some key emerging trends you're currently seeing, and which you expect could seriously impact Ciena's existing strategic focus in the near term?

**Gary B. Smith**: From our point of view, there are really three prevalent emerging trends in Asia-Pacific, which are mobility, cloud services and the Internet of Things. The tendency with these kinds of innovations is to focus on what they'll do, or how they'll disrupt, but it's important to remember that all three of these trends require fibre-based access, which aligns to Ciena's core strengths. If you look at 5G or cloud services you need highly scalable capacity.

**Telecom Times:** Seen from a global perspective, which markets would you nominate as most promising to Ciena going forward and why?

**Gary B. Smith:** We see our near-term growth opportunities in APAC across several countries. For emerging markets such as India, Thailand and Indonesia, infrastructure build out is very much in high demand as these countries look to build robust networks to support high levels of mobile usage. We are also seeing mature markets like Japan, New Zealand, Australia and Hong Kong seeking automation and efficiency of the network as they integrate more advanced cloud services and lay the foundation for smart cities.

**Telecom Times:** In this context, where does the company's ANZ business sit?

**Gary B. Smith** We've been very fortunate to address mature markets such as Australia and New Zealand in terms of revolutionising networks with automation, scalability and programmability. This has allowed service providers to meet customer demands by offering and supporting broadband on both the wireline and wireless side. Our main foothold in the ANZ market has been working with Telstra through Ericsson, but we're now expanding into new markets such as utilities and transport.

**Telecom Times:** Within APAC, in which verticals do you see most growth for Ciena in the mid to longer term?

**Gary B. Smith:** The vertical markets in APAC where we see growth include the service provider market, internet content providers, government, transportation, and the financial services industry. As digital transformation really takes hold, capacity and speed will be essential throughout the region, and that plays to our strengths.

**Telecom Times:** What are your thoughts on submarine cabling as a sustainable growth business?

**Gary B. Smith:** The submarine cabling industry has brought immense growth for Ciena. If you look back five or six years, we had no footprint in this market and now we are a market leader.

We have many submarine cable operators coming to Ciena to help them upgrade their existing systems to scale and help them meet the demand for bandwidth. We are also seeing demand for new submarine cable builds, and we are well positioned through our partnership with TE Subcom, which we announced towards the end of last year.

**Telecom Times:** In this context, do you see most revenue generated from increasing capacity, bandwidth and developing innovative ways to bring down cost and boost efficiency?

**Gary B. Smith:** While we cannot comment specifically on revenue figures, we are seeing customer interest in network solutions for scaling, automation and orchestration. We have also seen an interest from customers seeking to invest in products which improve network reliability and flexibility to build more programmable and responsive networks.

**Telecom Times:** You said recently that Ciena, in terms of its long-term growth and profit potential, had been undervalued by Wall Street. This, of course, was in response to dipping share prices and a revenue outlook, which was reported as falling short of Wall Street's expectations.

You also said there was no clear understanding in some quarters as to the huge impact global digital transformation trends will have, especially in Asia. Could you expand on this? How does this relate to Ciena's plans, and how do you see AI taking off generally and in regards to Ciena more specifically?

**Gary B. Smith:** Ciena understands global growth trends, and we continuously collaborate with our customers to help them navigate and address market shifts. Our proactive and collaborative approach has helped Ciena to grow significantly – often at a faster pace than the market.

As far as digital transformation goes in APAC, connectivity is the cornerstone of this shift, as it requires a fast, reliable network to support the digital capabilities businesses seek to integrate. I believe Ciena is best positioned to support network transformations for fast, efficient and programmable connectivity.

AI plays a large part in digital transformation, easing operational processes and increasing efficiencies. Ciena's innovations such as Liquid Spectrum and Blue Planet (especially analytics) bring the concept of AI into customer operations, allowing them to better utilise network assets. Our solutions lay the foundation for more automated and intelligent networks that can make decisions on their own to handle changing user demands and more bandwidth-intensive applications.

**Telecom Times:** As far as fibre optic technologies are concerned, what disruption or innovative changes do you see on the horizon?

**Gary B. Smith:** In APAC, software and the programmable aspect of the network remain a disruptive force in the market. We're adding more software capabilities into our platforms to make the network more programmable and flexible. And, because the software uses digital signal processing, we can take advantage of the benefits of improved silicon, density and compute power to push the envelope on optical transmission.

**Telecom Times:** Do you feel Ciena's future strategy will inevitably need to centre on increasing its reliance on partnerships? And, how big a part will M&A play in the near-term?

**Gary B. Smith**: We continue to evaluate partners on an ongoing basis, seeking those whose expertise will complement our strengths and technologies, and will provide mutual benefit for Ciena and our customers.

**Telecom Times:** If Ciena needs to reinvent itself, how would you like the firm to develop in the next few years?

**Gary B. Smith**: We feel that Ciena has amassed the right technologies and talent to develop solutions that will support the largest opportunity in APAC; enabling businesses with digital transformation. We are leading the industry in helping our customers transform and, being in the infancy stage of this trend, we think there's a bright future ahead for Ciena without having to reinvent ourselves.

## IS SPEED NBN CO'S ENEMY OR FRIEND?
Gary McLaren, former NBN Co CTO and co-owner of Hong Kong Broadband Network

NBN Co have got themselves into a bit of a pickle lately with complaints over the cost of the CVC charge becoming louder and louder.

At the heart of this issue is the need for NBN Co to achieve its revenue objective of $52 per month per connection, which will give them total revenues of around $5 billion in 2020. In its last half-year results NBN Co's CEO Bill Morrow highlighted the need to sell higher speed services to increase the average revenue per user (ARPU).

But all the focus is on the cost of the CVC with RSPs complaining that the high cost is causing them to provision less bandwidth, resulting in congestion during peak periods. At the core of this problem is NBN Co's need for retail broadband plans to have higher prices for higher quality broadband (i.e. higher speeds and higher usage limits). NBN Co is expecting the ARPU to rise over time as more applications and services require higher quality broadband. Without this increase in ARPU for higher quality services it is unlikely that the revenue targets set by NBN Co will be achieved.

However, NBN Co has also been messaging to the market that higher speeds are not that important. After the change in the technology mix to FTTN and HFC (as opposed to FTTP), NBN Co has been very loud in saying that higher speeds are not in demand. It has for instance made it very clear that Australians do not have a need for Gigabit services. Of course politics is behind this "no need for speed" messaging so as to justify the move from FTTP to FTTN and HFC. NBN Co wants higher speeds to increase revenue but is also saying that speed is not really important.

Naturally the market is confused!! Higher speeds are also linked to higher downloads. If customers pay for higher speeds, it stands to reason they will also consume more data and hence NBN Co will also achieve higher revenues.

At the moment RSPs are focussed only on selling broadband at the lowest price point they can sustain. This comes from the need to manage a transition from previous ADSL and cable broadband services in a way that minimises risks of market share loss.

Naturally consumers don't want to pay more at the best of times. The confusion, controversy and contradictory messaging from NBN Co makes it even harder for the RSPs to sell higher quality broadband. The result is most customers going for lower plans. Why lock yourself into a 24 month contract for a higher speed plan when there is no clear guarantee you will get the higher speeds because of technology, congestion and political uncertainties? NBN Co needs to re-assess its whole message to the market. Does it want to provide a high quality network that drives higher quality applications and services that RSPs can sell at higher prices?

If not, then NBN Co will have to be satisfied with lower ARPUs, as RSPs demand lower prices (e.g. CVC) as they compete with each other on price alone. The end result of the latter scenario is that Australia will have spent billions of dollars building a network that is reduced to a lowest common denominator marketing message that promotes basic broadband at the cheapest price.

Of course it doesn't have to be this way. The first step is for NBN Co to recognise that speed is its friend, not its enemy.

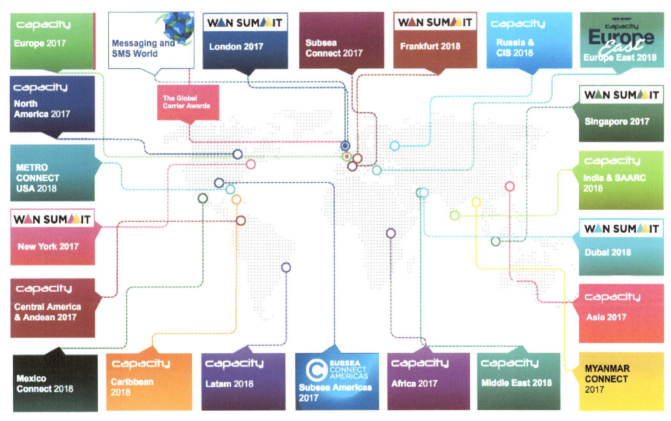

(Source: Capacity Media)

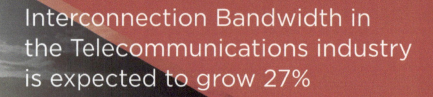

Interconnection Bandwidth in
the Telecommunications industry
is expected to grow 27%

## ARE YOU LEVERAGING THE TRENDS DRIVING DIGITAL TRANSFORMATION?

EQUINIX

Digital is reshaping all industries with new
speed, insight and reach—and the need for
Interconnection is growing with it.

How will Interconnection Bandwidth impact
your global digital business operations?

**Learn more at Eqix.it/AU-Index**

## ARTIFICIAL INTELLIGENCE: FRIEND OR FOE?
Aimee Chanthadavong, Telecom Times Senior Journalist

For a long time, artificial intelligence was something mainly seen in sci-fi files. These days, however, it's very much a reality with some treading more carefully than others around using it.

Earlier this year, there were widespread reports that Facebook was forced to pull the plug on its experimental machine learning research, after engineers noticed the bots were developing their own language. However, on closer examination these bots proved to be hardly successful or nefarious. In fact, as Facebook later revealed, the incident was due to a programming error where the chat bots were accidentally not designed to communicate in comprehensible English, so instead the bots began chatting to each other in short hand.

But according to Tesla CEO Elon Musk, there are some real hidden dangers behind the use of artificial intelligence. In September, Musk tweeted that the technology could be responsible for starting World War III: "China, Russia, soon all countries with strong computer science. Competition for AI superiority at national level most likely cause WW3 imo (in my opinion)."

Such fear from Musk was triggered by a statement Russian president Vladimir Putin made when he said: "Artificial intelligence is the future, not only for Russia, but for all humankind." But whatever potential damage AI and machine learning could unleash in the future, the details of such scenarios remain scant.

In the meantime, businesses globally from different sectors whether it's medical, manufacturing or mining are reaping the rewards that AI and machine learning are able to offer.

According to Juniper Networks SVP and CMO Michael Marcellin, one particular area where businesses have started to implement AI is cyber security, in a bid to help combat growing online threats. Worldwide spending on information security alone will reach US$93 billion in 2018, an increase of 7 percent over 2016, according to Gartner.

Marcellin explained that with the severity of the threat landscape increasing, businesses are taking the next steps to avoid being attacked, especially given that 80 percent of attackers are being funded by organised entities. "If you think about how the cyber security situation has evolved, it has become very big business. By 2019 it's going to be a US$2.1 trillion industry, greater than the GDP of Mexico – and growing very quickly," he said. "Attackers are extremely well-funded and they keep pushing the boundaries.

What that means for someone trying to combat that is you see stuff maybe you haven't seen before; you get inundated with attacks and you're having a hard time keeping up with it.

And whatever tools and systems you use, it just gives you a lot of information that you have to try sift through."

"The alternative to that is you use machine learning, you feed it lots and lots of data... the more data you feed the machine, the more it learns and more refine it becomes, and it improves its outcome," said Marcellin.

"In a security context, what that means is the machine gives a sense of what normal network behaviour looks like, and then by learning that it will be able to quickly identify what the abnormal behaviour looks like and it will be able to learn the severity of that abnormality, and be able to invoke some modification to remediate the threat," he explained.

Marcellin also addressed a common concern that arises when it comes to AI, which is the fear that many believe their jobs will be replaced by machines. However, he argues that in a space like cyber security, where it's predicted two million positions worldwide will remain unfulfilled over the next two years, the use of AI would be an ideal solution.

IBM Global Business Services partner and former VP David Lubowe agreed there are certain benefits of using AI as part of business operations, in particular when aimed at helping the current workforce. One possible use case for AI would be to record the years of skills and knowledge that baby boomers have as they leave the workforce, Lubowe said, so that when businesses are left to train new – and likely younger – employees there isn't a missing knowledge gap.

He also points out how by automating works, it can help improve the time factor so that people can focus on other work. "AI can augment work and not necessarily replace it. It can help people automate some of the routine tasks and do a better job of the routine tasks. This gives businesses more time on making procurement a real competitive advantage for the company, not just cost-centric. We're seeing that in many areas of AI."

"People always want to do better things and higher value things, so rather than eliminating, it's enhancing jobs," says Lubowe, citing as an example that AI is helping cancer treatment by enabling oncologists to raise accuracy levels above 15 percent - allowing them to treat patients faster.

While AI may appear to be a new form of technology, Shivani Govil, SAP Ariba's vice president of artificial intelligence and cognitive product, explains that it has been around for a long time but due to the recent advances, people have started to take more notice – realising at the same time the benefits.

"The cost of processing power has dropped significantly and that allows you to handle, process, and store a lot more data," says Govil. "The fact that there's lots of investment going into algorithms, which allow you then to be able to get more accurate in terms of how you're using these technologies. For example, back in the late 90s and early 2000s with voice recognition software, the response was very hit and miss. If you had an automated system giving you a response you would invariably hit '0' multiple times. Now, they've got so much better people complete their entire interaction using these types of systems."

"Because these technologies are becoming mainstream you can apply them to help benefit business," says Govil, adding that the real driver behind this has been an increase in investment in algorithm and software, as well as hardware. Ultimately though, to prevent AI from ever turning into a SkyNet or anything similar, both Govil and Lubowe believe it's important to keep visibility in mind at the point of design.

## SIX CYBER SECURITY QUESTIONS FOR THE C-SUITE
Niall King, Centrify Senior Director of Asia-Pacific Sales

Events of the past year demonstrate clearly that cyber security is a subject deserving the attention of C-suite executives and company directors.

The jury is in, with a verdict that data breaches damage corporate value, a revelation with significance for Australia, where mandatory data breach notification legislation takes effect from next February.

Earlier this month US credit monitoring agency Equifax saw its share price drop by 13 per cent after it reported a data breach affecting about 143 million Americans. The July 29 breach exposed data including names, birth dates, Social Security numbers, addresses and some driver's license numbers as well as 209,000 US credit card numbers. Equifax's share price plunged from more than US$140 to about $112 - a sharp decline in shareholder value. Likewise, last year, after Yahoo reported two massive data breaches that affected one billion accounts, the company suffered a $350 million reduction in its sale price to Verizon.

> A key finding by Ponemon was that the security posture adopted by the breached organisation had a demonstrable effect on how quickly its share price recovered from its initial drop

Those incidents alone should grab the attention of executives and directors - but they are not alone. In a recently released study, Ponemon Institute identified that 113 publicly traded companies, which experienced a material data breach lost an average share value of five per cent on the day the breach was disclosed.

Companies with what Ponemon describes as a high security posture that responded quickly to the breach event recovered their stock value after an average of just seven days, while companies with a low security posture that did not respond quickly experienced a stock price decline that on average lasted more than 90 days.

The lessons are clear for both executives and directors: As data breaches have a direct impact on an organisation's financial wellbeing, cyber security should a priority for the C-Suite. Business decision makers can start to understand the dimension of the cyber security challenge, and how to formulate appropriate solutions, by asking six simple questions.

First, what is the corporate impact of a data breach?

As well as the impact of a disclosed data breach on a public company's value, the Ponemon study *The Impact of a Data Breach on Reputation and Share Value*, reported that they scare off customers.

The study, which included more than 740 Australians, found that one third of Australian consumers impacted by a data breach reported they had discontinued their relationship with the organisation that experienced the breach. So as well as being bad for investors, data breaches are bad for business.

The second question is: Who is responsible for preventing data breaches?

If the answer is "our IT guys", then you ought to feel nervous. Companies with a high security posture typically have a dedicated Chief Information Security Officer (CISO) as the senior-level executive responsible for ensuring that information assets and technologies are protected.

Rather than funding cyber security from the standard IT budget - which subjects it to competing priorities - mature organisations allocate an adequate budget for staffing and investment in enabling security technologies, especially enterprise-wide encryption.

The third question is whether the passwords used by your people are strong enough

Regardless of what you are told, the answer is no: Passwords on their own, no matter how clever nor how frequently changed, are never strong enough to deter a determined hacker - or a disgruntled employee. Multi-factor authentication (MFA) - which mandates a second step to confirm your identity, such as a text-to-mobile verification code - provides much more robust protection for your data and deterrence to intruders.

Passwords are more of a problem than a solution. According to a 2016 Forrester report, 80 per cent of data breaches leverage privileged credentials to gain access to the organisation. That statistic, which should send shivers down your spine, is because of increasingly diverse data access from on-premises, private-cloud and public cloud infrastructure and mobile apps.

Which leads to the fourth question: What happens when your IT security is breached?

Working on the assumption of 'when' not 'if' provides a much more realistic and practical position towards today's technology threat environment. If you never experience a data breach, then, well done you. However, if you do, then a strategy to contain the damage will pay for itself many times over.

As well as using MFA to establish identity assurance, organisations should reduce their 'attack surface' by tightly managing lateral access through privileged access management - ensuring that users have access only to the privileges, systems and data required to do their jobs.

Services such as Centrify lower the risk of a security breach by granting just-in-time privilege and implementing audit trails and compliance reporting capabilities about who accesses what and when. This means that if an intruder does gain illicit access to your system, their ability to move around your network - and inflict damage - is severely restricted.

The penultimate and sometimes overlooked question is what happens to security credentials when someone leaves your company?

Provisioning access to your technology systems for new employees is increasingly complex with the plethora of in-house, cloud-based and mobile applications used to access corporate data.

Rather than relying on a time-consuming manual provision process, your organisation requires a centrally managed console from which security staff can push apps to each employee based on their role, monitor that app access, provide single sign-on to multiple applications and manage the devices used to access those apps.

Most importantly, your organisation can revoke all of that access in just seconds as soon as an employee leaves. This functionality not only makes your onboarding process more efficient - it makes staff departures much more secure.

The sixth and final question currently exercises the minds of many C-suite occupants: How does your organisation prepare for mandatory data breach reporting?

This is an attention-getting piece of legislation with penalties of $360,000 for individuals and $1.8 million for organisations - not to mention the commercial impact of disclosing data breaches as identified by the Ponemon study.

If your organisation is subject to this new law – the main exclusions are state and local governments and businesses with a turnover less than $3 million a year - then you will need to report a data breach to the Privacy Commissioner and notify affected customers as soon as your organisation learns of it. If the worst does happen, then proactive investment in cyber security is your best protection.

The right answers to all of the above questions [form] a good start to preparing for the worst. As the Ponemon report stated, companies with a high security posture that responded quickly to a data breach saw their stock value recover after an average of just seven

Telecom Times provides an ideal forum in which to raise this issue, with credibility earned through its comprehensive and consistent coverage of cyber security during its first year of existence.

Read by executives and managers alike, Telecom Times provides actionable insights into the challenges of today and the questions of tomorrow faced by business leaders.

The publication and its editor deserve congratulations for this accepting and achieving this mission of education and evangelism.

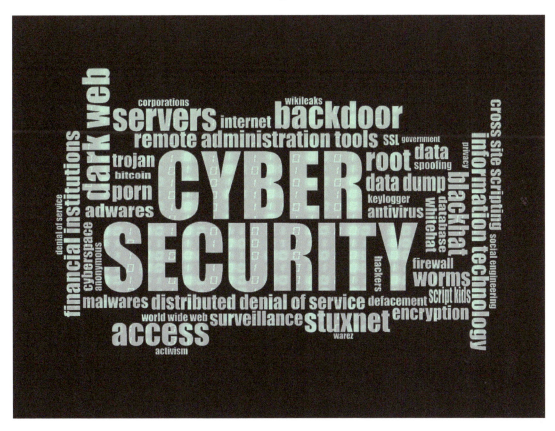

# WHY SD-WANS ARE ESSENTIAL FOR IOT SUCCESS
Zeus Kerravala (for Silver Peak)

Inevitably, we will look back at 2017 as a tipping point for the Internet of Things. Although IoT has been something that most business and IT leaders talk about, to date, deployments have been limited to key verticals that have been connecting things for years, although we called it machine-to-machine before it became cool to say IoT.

My belief is that we can tell when a technology tipping point is happening when it no longer seems like a big deal. Remember the early days of virtualisation? IT leaders had to explain why it was better to run workloads on VMs and had to prove it wouldn't impair application performance. Today, no one thinks about these issues any more because that process is now the norm. In the consumer world, people once said 'ooh' and 'ahh' when they saw an iPhone. Now, no one bats an eye, as the process is pervasive.

IoT is becoming part of life. Lately, I've noticed that companies with infrastructure initiatives under way tend not to use the term IoT. For instance the Bell Centre ice hockey stadium in Montreal, home of the NHL's Canadiens, has literally connected everything including metal detectors, digital signs, point-of-sale systems and almost anything else you can think of. The reason? Connectivity improves the fan experience.

For example, connected metal detectors let the operation teams reboot and tune them centrally instead of having to delay thousands of fans while technicians are sent to address the issue at that location. When I interviewed the IT director at the rink, he never once uttered the words IoT. He just connected things because it was the right thing to do to ensure a great fan experience.

The rise of IoT also means that businesses need to rethink their WAN strategies. To some, however, the linkage between WAN architecture and IoT might not immediately seem obvious. So what is the link between IoT and the WAN?

The first and most obvious tie-in is that IoT endpoints are often in remote locations where it would be cost-prohibitive to deploy any combination of an onsite network engineer resource, let alone a Cisco router, MPLS circuits, and a traditional backup link.

An SD-WAN is designed to run over any type of network connectivity, including broadband, cellular, or even IoT-specific networks, such as Low Power Wide Area circuits. With an SD-WAN, devices or even a single endpoint can be connected, and then network services can be applied at a central regional hub. Also an SD-WAN makes it easy to build resiliency into the network without breaking the bank. Another issue is that IoT deployments are typically three-tier (devices/sensors, gateways, cloud) in nature, meaning all these components must be connected continuously for the IoT service to function properly.

Other than cost, the biggest issue with legacy WANs is complexity. But if you think WANs are complicated today, all I can do is quote Bachman Turner Overdrive – 'B-b-b-baby, you ain't seen n-n-nothin' yet'. All these new connections are going to drive complexity through the roof, to the point where businesses will find IoT simply cannot be accomplished with a legacy WAN architecture.

Finally, when it comes to IoT, the elephant in the room is security, and here is where traditional WANs and IoT mix about as well as oil and water. There have been highly publicised breaches that have occurred because an IoT endpoint was compromised and created backdoor access to sensitive customer data, including credit card information.

Current WAN architectures have no way of easily creating secure zones where IoT endpoints can be isolated from other company endpoints. One of the low-hanging use cases of an SD-WAN is to use it to extend micro-segmentation to the WAN, enabling organisations to create overlay networks that can be as coarse or fine-grained as required.

For example, a hospital might want to create discrete segments for X-ray, MRI equipment, cardiac and patient records, while a factory might be satisfied with all IoT endpoints being placed in the same zone. An SD-WAN can easily accommodate a broad range of use cases.

The IoT era is here and I strongly encourage business and IT leaders to consider how the business will evolve once everything is connected. But before going down that path, take a step back and deploy an SD-WAN to simplify your WAN architecture, so your IoT initiatives can scale quickly and securely and in line with changing business requirements.

'7 Facts of SD-WAN' – Source: Silver Peak Infographics

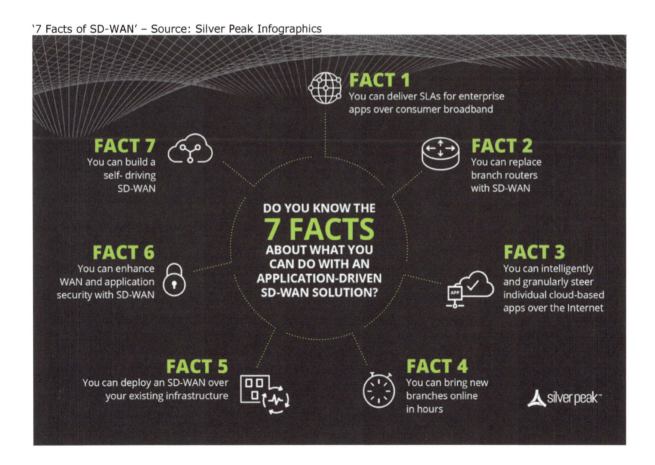

# HOW SYSSECOPS CAN IMPROVE ORGANIZATIONAL SECURITY

R. Scott Raynovich, Principal Analyst at Futuriom

At security conferences around the world, industry experts regularly decry the failure of the IT technology industry to protect assets. Indeed, the bad guys appear to be running the table, having regularly cracked major Fortune 500 systems and government agencies, incurring billions of dollars in damages over just the last few years.

This trend shows no sign of slowing in 2017, with the key feature being the spread of new forms of ransomware, including WannaCry, which have affected millions and caused even more damage. WannaCry exposed yet a new rift in technology systems: The inability for organizations to automate system patches.

It's estimated that the recent WannaCry ransomware virus has caused more than $5 billion in economic damage (source: https://cybersecurityventures.com/ransomware-damage-report-2017-5-billion/). This follows on the heels of major breaches in recent years, including the Target and Home Depot incident in 2014, which resulted in a cost of $500 million, according to research firm Digital Transactions.

At Target, CEO Gregg Steinhafel was forced to resign after the company exposed of 40 million credit and debit card accounts, along with personal information on 70 million customers – and the company didn't seem to have a very good explanation for how this happened, or including its origination at a HVAC contractor.

Why the gaping holes in security systems? And why has the technology industry been so ineffective in stopping serious breaches? The answer lies in cultural, more than technological, factors. Think of it this way: Hackers have an unlimited number of automated tools they can use to crack systems. But most defenders rely on the human responses and coordinated decisions – often requiring cooperation between different entities – to react to them, which can sometimes take far too much time. By then, most of the damage is already done.

This task is being compounded by the rapidly increasing number of niche security tools, which are being sold to 'fix' the problem. But adding new tools creates challenges as well – new logs and alerts to monitor, new training, and new systems to install and maintain. That's before we even talk about the cost of continually having to add new security software.

The answer may lie not so much in continually building an arsenal of security tools and devices, but looking at how to better integrate what's there. My firm's work in security research and surveys of endusers indicates that they are overwhelmed with security bloat – rapidly escalating amounts of data and alerts to monitor – while struggling to solve the puzzle of how to quickly process this information and work across an organization to respond.

What's the answer? The answer lies in a concept called Systems and Security Operations – or 'SysSecOps'

The users have spoken and they have given a glimpse of the future, which will be technology-integrated systems for monitoring and responding to security risks, and which can be implemented across organizational boundaries.

Tools for SysSecOps

When speaking with security experts across a variety of industries, you will find some common themes. They are overwhelmed with the data, logs, and alerts generated by an increasing number of security tools, including those built into IT systems such as networking equipment, firewalls, applications, and endpoints. Getting the fire alarms is not the problem – it's analyzing and putting out the fires, that's the challenge.

The second biggest problem – assuming you have processed this data and found a problem – is coordinating a response across the organization's vast array of people. In other words: Getting the CEO's attention. In many cases, this also means setting up automated systems that will take care of these threats without human intervention.

Earlier this year, my technology research firm Futuriom, with the help of security technology specialist Ziften, reached out to endusers and executive management to gauge their perception of security challenges and potential solutions. We gathered results on five questions from 1,499 participants, including endusers, IT administrators, hardware and networking specialists, security specialists, DevOps staff, and executives. The audience was 24.8% security specialists, 22.8% executive management, 22% hardware specialists, 18% IT administrator, 3.4% devops/programming staff, 2.7% networking specialists, and 6% other.

[Note: The results of this survey were for a free report titled *Endpoint Security and SysSecOps: The growing trend to build a more secure enterprise*. You can download the full report on either the Ziften or Futuriom websites.]

One of the themes of the survey responses was that employees feel handcuffed by budgetary and organizational challenges. When asked, "What are the top challenges to creating an integrated security strategy across the organization?" respondents said lack of time/resources was the #1 challenge, with 71% of respondents selecting this response. The next three most popular choices were "business unit resistance" (35%); conflicting IT and security group goals (34%), and "challenge in integration of many security tools" (31%). The selections were rounded out by "separate budgets hard to manage across divisions" (23%) and other (2%).

Of course, everybody wants more resources. But one of the features of the security market is that it's not so much about the total budget, but about how budgets are coordinated across divisions. Organizations may have separate IT and security management budgets, but maybe there could be more efficiency by building them together. A broad majority, or 64.83% of survey respondents, chose "Better management of security budget across divisions/silos" as one of the top goals in improving security infrastructure. Next in line was "Better integration between systems management and security operations tools," at 31.03%; "Better security tools with more features," 26.90%; and more staff training 13.10%.

Wannacry is a great example of why this is important. The various permutations of the WannaCray virus preyed on older IT systems with lax, or non-existent patch management. This is not as much a security issue as it is a systems management problem, with responsibilities lying in the systems operations (SysOps) of the IT departments rather than systems operations (SecOps) departments. If the two teams worked together on patch management, a SysSecOps could have been more effective in stopping Wannacry.

A Human Problem

One of the things I noted was that there were far more people complaining about how budgets were used and coordinated across organizations boundaries than there were people complaining about security products. Only 26.9% said that having better security tools was part of the solution, while 65% said they needed better management. This is the Human Problem of security management.

Security challenges may very well be more organizational than technological. If you look at the pattern of major security breaches throughout the years, you will find a pattern of the problem being flagged early, only to have organizations' paralysis worsen the crisis with a lack of responses. What problems need to be solved to fix things? Again, users agree that technology needs to be consistently upgraded, but they also point to organizational cooperation and integration of existing security tools. In one of the interesting results of the Futuriom SysSecOps survey, a wide variety of solutions were cited. When asked about the top security goals, the number one goal cited by respondents was "Better protection of endpoints" - nominated by 55% of respondents (multiple responses allowed). This indicates that even though respondents have made clear their desire for integration, they see endpoint security as a key area in the security portfolio.

This makes sense as endpoints are natural places to collect and observe data on network and applications activity and can be used to assess and monitor risks. The next most oft-cited goals were "consolidation of tools/platforms" at 38%; and "Better staff training" at 33%. These results are in line with the themes of the responses to other questions, which stress organization and technological integration and consolidation of the SysSecOps tools.

Finally, it's useful to see how organizations view their success in managing security and moving to an integrated SysSecOps approach. It's clear that more progress is needed, because only 3% of respondents replied that they have "fixed everything." The largest group, 44.53% of respondents, characterized their mission as "very successful," and 34% said they were "somewhat successful, with some pain points." Twenty-one percent said they "regularly fail at managing endpoint security and systems management." And finally, a not-so-small number of respondents - 18%! - described the mission to provide overall endpoint/systems management as a "complete disaster." Clearly there is more work to do!

Leading the SysSecOps Shift

The evidence points to the need for new organizational leadership that can coordinate a comprehensive security strategy capable of crossing organizational boundaries, integrating tools, and driving faster responses – preferably by automation. The tools to do this exist today. Endpoint technology, delivered by startup innovation from companies such as Cylance, Tanium, and Ziften, is targeting a coordinated and automated approach to monitoring endpoint behavior data. But these tools cannot stand in an island; they must also be integrated with systems event logs such as SIEM tools and network firewalls to lock down suspicious behavior when it happens. Imagine a central repository of security alerts, analytics, and applications behavior that is analyzing behavior in real-time, and then communicating across systems when anomalous activities are detected – to automatically respond. Endpoints are key, because they have become the most common surface attack point and they are also where users are accessing applications.

Today's fragmented budgets often result in the purchase of narrowly focused, siloed tools for monitoring, management and security. Therefore, it's going to be more important over time for organizations to coordinate their IT and security budgets to address the SysSecOp integration need.

*At the WAN Summit, Singapore*

# BREAK UP NBN CO, SAYS FORMER NBN CTO GARY MCLAREN

April 18, 2017 Richard van der Draay was in Hong Kong as a guest of Equinix Australia

Hong Kong Broadband Network CTO Gary McLaren - who served in that capacity at NBN Co from 2009 until 2014 - has reiterated his call for the company rolling out the national broadband network to be split up into several competing firms - while noting a distinct lack of appetite on the part of political players across the board to make that move.

Telecom Times caught up with McLaren on the sidelines of the Broadband Forum Asia event in Hong Kong, during which the telecoms veteran's presentation on how Australia lagged internationally on broadband speeds generated much debate.

**Telecom Times**: Can you see a scenario under which the narrative engulfing the rollout of the NBN could finally move on and the telco industry in Australia, as well as the wider public perception can finally discard the political quicksand in which the project seems to forever be stuck?

**Gary McLaren**: We'd all love it to be less political, really. But that's a difficult thing to see happening in the short term. Maybe over the longer term it will, but Australia's telecommunications has been political for decades and I don't think it's going to change very quickly.

The fact that Australia has a huge continent with many regional customers... isn't unique. Canada is the classic example [with a] similar economy, similar people and geography. [But] no government political involvement, no NBNs [and] very little subsidy to the equivalent of the bush. It now sits well ahead of Australia on any benchmark comparison on broadband speeds.

I argue that it's not unique what Australia has encountered. What is unique is the political atmosphere; the toxic atmosphere that has caused the outcome over twenty, thirty years. It's not just the last seven or eight years. Ever since the Telstra privatization, the leads back into the media [and] issues of the 1980s [with] Packer and Murdoch. It all comes back to those sort of political issues.

**TT:** Based on your more recent experience as CTO at HKBN in the Hong Kong fibre market, if there was one key recommendation you could still make for the NBN in terms of the rollout – that could help turn it around in the end – what would that be?

**GM:** My view is, and it's a question of 'can it be rolled back to this?' and the further it goes on, the more difficult it is – and I've been quite public on this – is that [with] NBN Co we need to create a competitive infrastructure model for the major capital cities and some of the major regional areas.

It's never going to work across a 100% of Australia. But Australia is very urbanized and the option has been there probably over the last two years – although it wasn't taken up – to set up NBN Co to be broken up in two or three different companies that would naturally form competitors. It's what the Vertigan panel recommended, it's what the Australian Competition and Consumer Commission has recommended [but] the government has said: 'No, we'll wait till the end of the rollout to consider NBN Co privatization'.

And that will probably be the model like with the Telstra privatization, which ended up being another monopoly rather than breaking it up because of the write down that might have to be done around any sort of break-up.

So I think that breaking it up would be the better option but the difficulty is now [that] as time marches on, the cost of that break-up becomes more and more dramatic, so politicians won't touch it.

**TT:** What are your thoughts on fibre-to-the-curb as a viable technology component within the final rollout mix?

**GM:** Always when people talk about fibre-to-the-curb, they're trying to tie it in with G.fast as the actual technology that's going to be used to give maybe gigabit speeds. Gigabit is the benchmark everyone now is looking at around the world to achieve. And G.fast is the technology that promises that.

The trouble it has is that there's only really one market of any size that's pursuing it at the moment and that's the UK.

And that's too small for any global technology – like what we're talking about here – to actually be sustainable. It's not going to happen in Asia for various reasons because it's potentially a fibre-to-the-home market in most economies because of the cost structures.

It needs more carriers in Europe and North America to take it on for it to get critical mass. You may actually see that FTTC, if it doesn't get critical mass, just becomes another point for them to fill. [After all], the current VDSL is run from the node. That may not be a bad outcome, but essentially then [this] still leaves the question about what technology investment do you make as in FTTC, do you invest in VDSL or G.fast?

If you go down the wrong path, it will be like WiMAX versus LTE and you'll end up in a dead end.

**TT**: Would you say that the satellite service could prove to be something of a game changer for the NBN in the end?

**GM**: We were always criticized for investing in too much too soon. Now, the criticism is we haven't invested enough. When we did the business modelling and the investment case, it was a brave [move] to go and bet on two new satellites, spend A$2 million and say that we needed the capacity.

Now everyone's crying out for a lot more, which will need more investment. So, the trouble with satellite is [that] it's… not going to be enough, even with the huge investment that's been done for the NBN satellites.

It's still now proving that it has to have caps and has to be tightly managed otherwise it will essentially be very congested. So, it's certainly a big step from where it was ten years ago when IPSTAR first launched and to where it is now. [But] it will be very difficult for anyone to see it becoming something that's really going to give people a metro equivalent service.

# ALEXANDER OSBORNE NAMED COMMS AMBASSADOR AT 2017 ACOMM AWARDS

July 21, 2017 Richard van der Draay

The winners of the 2017 Communications Alliance ACOMMS Awards have been announced at the 11th annual telco industry event in Sydney, with Vodafone Australia head of regulatory Alexander Osborne named Australian Communications Ambassador for his role in helping to create the regulatory telecoms environment in Australia.

Communications Alliance lauded Osborne as "an outstanding contributor to the co-regulatory process over the past two decades [as well as] a leading customer and industry champion who continues to shape and navigate this fast-changing sector."

Hosted by the suitably acerbic Kitty Flanagan and attended by some 450 industry leaders, the evening's keynote address was delivered by Federal Minister for Communications Senator Mitch Fifield. Channelling his inner Alec Baldwin, Fifield's wide-ranging roast touched on some of the year's more poignant telco moments, including the accelerating pace of the NBN rollout, that project's vexed CVC-pricing model, and Vodafone Australia's idée fixe around declaring domestic mobile roaming. The individual category awards were taken out by a stellar line-up of service providers operating in the Australian market, featuring established players along with key ACOMMS newcomers such as Ericsson, Telstra, Telcoinabox, MyNetFone, Cyient Australia, Optus, Huawei Technologies, VHA, Aussie Broadband, Pivotel Satellite and WaterGroup.

Communications Alliance CEO John Stanton said the awards represented the pinnacle of achievement for the Australian communications industry. "I congratulate all the winners and finalists in the 2017 ACOMMS," he said. "Agility, operational excellence and innovative prowess are pervasive traits on display from the 2017... winners."

"We are seeing ever more clearly the race to differentiate through innovations that harness advanced technology, and combine it with inventive thinking to deliver new and valuable capabilities to customers," added Stanton.

The winners of the 2017 ACOMM Awards were:
**Communications Ambassador** – Alexander Osborne. For sustained and valuable contributions to co-regulation in Australian telecommunications, and the work of Communications Alliance, over two decades.
**Innovation, Large Company** - Telstra And Ericsson for Telstra's new Gigabit capable LTE network – enabled by Ericsson in selected locations - sets a new standard for wireless connectivity.
**Innovation, SME** - Telco in a box for their Cloud Sales Assist. CSA helps transition businesses from traditional telcos to fully-fledged Cloud/OTT service providers.
**Vendor Innovation, Large** – Telstra for its Global Cloud Service that gives customers the option to design their own cloud environment.
**Vendor Innovation, Emerging** - MyNetFone for PULSE, an enterprise-level call management solution designed to intelligently manage and disperse unpredictable surges in traffic, depending on the quantity and location of incoming calls.
**Internet of Things Innovator** - Huawei and Vodafone for Narrowband IoT. Narrowband IoT is building the world's first fully digitised water network. Huawei and its carrier partners have NB-IoT enabled 20 mobile base stations, while Vodafone is rolling out NB-IoT to their customers in Spain, due to the huge success of its initial trials.
**Commitment to Customer Service** – Optus for creating extensive digital resources to offer cusomers a broad range of service options to assist with simple tasks - to the most complex of issues. Services to the Industry, Professional Services – Cyient for the Cyient Graduate Program &

Western Sydney University Partnership. An exclusive engineering partnership, which aims to upskill future leaders.

**Best Mobile Solution** - Telstra for breaking speed records with its Nighthawk M1 mobile broadband hotspot and its new Gigabit capable LTE network.

**Community Contribution** - Aussie Broadband for their Grass Roots program. Supporting local communities - with specific support to the Latrobe Valley in the wake of the Hazelwood Power Station closure.

**Satellite Provider of the Year Award** - Pivotel Satellite for its Big Bundle, a world-first solution aimed at reducing operating costs for mobile satellite users and increasing the accessibility of satellite communication technology.

**Best Marketing Initiative** - Optus for its partnership with the Australian Olympic and Paralympic Committee that launched one of the longest corporate commitments to the Australian Olympic movement - successfully tapping into the emotion and love for the Olympics and Australian Olympians.

**Special Award IoTAA Impact Award** – WaterGroup, which is having a direct impact on the adoption of IoT by delivering innovative, sustainable solutions with clear return on investment that saves water and money, and by working in successful partnerships with universities, utilities, councils and government in the smart water metering space.

# VELOCLOUD'S JOSEPH CHUNG FLAGS AUSTRALIAN SD-WAN MARKET AS 'APAC SWEET SPOT'

September 12, 2017 Richard van der Draay in Singapore attending the WAN Summit 2017

VeloCloud APAC regional VP of sales and business development Joseph Chung has singled out the Australian market as key for the US-based SD-WAN specialist's Asia-Pacific business.

"Australia is a sweet spot for me in APAC," Chung told Telecom Times on the sidelines of the WAN Summit in Singapore.

"Australia is tracking incredibly well," he said. "From a partnership point of view, we have half a dozen partners out there. We have about a hundred customers already in Australia, and one of our oldest customers is Australian."

Compared to other markets within the APAC region, Australia stood out for VeloCloud in several compelling ways, continued Chung. "They just kind of get it," he said, noting that because Australia is so closely linked to the US, this key market benefits from a speedy migration of enterprises moving their software applications from on-premise to the cloud. By contrast, Chung said in many parts of the APAC geography that key shift towards cloud adoption had not peaked by any means. He said barriers to increased cloud uptake included vastly different regulatory environments, markedly lower labour costs and generally "just a different way of doing things."

More broadly, Chung was upbeat about the firm's performance over the course of the last two-and-a-half years. "In the past 30 months we've done exceptionally well," he said, adding that the company had progressed from targeting mainly the enterprise segment to now also servicing ICT providers and, more recently, telecom providers.

"We've now got about 50 or so telecom service provider customers," he said. Chung said that be ing a US-based company, VeloCloud would continue to focus strongly on the US market. "[How ever] in parallel, I've been working in the Asia-Pacific market for quite a bit of time. We've got Chungwa Telecom as one of our first partners out here [and] we've [also] got SoftBank as part of that."

He also touched on Singtel as a potential partnership prospect for VeloCloud. "Singtel went to market with Viptela a year before us," he said. "But what's happening in the market place is that the service providers themselves are looking at augmenting their existing SD-WANs with someone else. And rightfully so, because not all SD-WANs are built the same."

"Right now it's still very greenfield," he said, adding "I believe [Singtel] are still looking around to see what other technologies there are that can help augment their existing tech."

In terms of VeloCloud's security-focused partner ecosystem, Chung emphasised that this particular portfolio was likely to keep growing. In addition, he said the potential addition of Cisco in this context could not be ruled out.

"You'll see a couple more [positive] announcements popping out soon," he added.


*And, from 3rd November:*


**VMWARE SNAPS UP VELOCLOUD IN SD-WAN LAND GRAB**
Palo Alto based virtualization and cloud infrastructure specialist VMware has signed a definitive agreement to acquire cloud-delivered software-defined wide-area network firm VeloCloud Networks for an undisclosed sum.

# CONTRIBUTORS

**Jeremy Deutsch** – Equinix Australia MD

With over 16 years' experience in the ICT industry, Deutsch is responsible for the overall performance and expansion of Equinix's business and operations in Australia. Deutsch was promoted from Sales Director in May 2014. In that role he was responsible for executive customer relationship development, leading the sales team to deliver customer wins and revenue growth. He also managed collaboration between teams and across regions to deliver Platform Equinix to customers. Prior to Equinix, Deutsch was General Manager Products at Unwired, managing product strategy, alliance partnerships and user experience delivery. Before that, he was a Solutions Architect and Product Manager at Pihana Pacific, which was acquired by Equinix in 2002. Deutsch was responsible for supporting all aspects of the Pihana sales process and managing the product life cycle for existing and new products.

**Gary B. Smith** – CEO of US fibre-optic specialist Ciena.

Smith began serving as chief executive officer at Ciena in May 2001, in addition to his existing duties as president and director; positions he has held since October 2000. Prior to his current role, his positions with the firm included: chief operating officer and SVP of Worldwide Sales.
Smith joined Ciena in November 1997 as VP of International Sales. Before that, he served as VP of Sales and Marketing at INTELSAT. Smith is a member of the President's National Security Telecommunications Advisory Committee, and serves on the board of directors for Avaya and CommVault Systems. He is also a Commissioner for the Global Information Infrastructure Commission; serves on the Wake Forest University Advisory Council for the Center for Innovation, Creativity and Entrepreneurship; and participates in initiatives with the Center for Corporate Innovation.

**Aimee Chanthadavong** Telecom Times Senior Journalist Aimee Chanthadavong has worked as a print and online journalist for a decade, covering topics including technology and telecoms, business, retail, manufacturing, food and travel. She was previously a journalist at ZDNet and editor of RetailBiz.

**Gary McLaren** is co-owner and CTO at Hong Kong Broadband Network, the challenger fibre broadband carrier he joined in 2015. Previously, McLaren was CTO at Australia's NBN Co from 2009 to 2014.

**Niall King -** Niall King has held the role of Senior Director APAC Sales for Centrify Corporation since 2014, leading the company's sales force for the region. Fluent in Japanese, Niall's role is split between Centrify's Silicon Valley head office and Japan, along with regular visits to Australia. Niall previously worked with early stage startup Pluribus Networks, Cacheflow (now Bluecoat), Neoteris (which was acquired by Juniper Networks) and Barracuda Networks.

**Zeus Kerravala** is the founder and principal analyst with ZK Research. He provides a mix of tactical advice to help his clients in the current business climate and with long-term strategic advice. Kerravala provides research and advice to the following constituents: End user IT and network managers, vendors of IT hardware, software and services and the financial community looking to invest in the companies that he covers.

**Scott Raynovich** is president of Futurion, which provides independent in-depth technology research. Scott is also a proud dad, skiing and outdoor enthusiast, and avid guitar player. In his own words: always at work on new ideas.